WAVES OF HOPE

Waves of Hope

Published by
Top Down Press

ISBN: 978-1-7355551-0-2
eISBN: 978-1-7355551-1-9

Cover Artwork by Carol Comins

DEDICATION

THIS BOOK IS DEDICATED TO THE FAMILIES AND
DESCENDANTS OF THE AMERICAN PRISONERS OF
WORLD WAR II

WAVES OF HOPE

TABLE OF CONTENTS

FOREWORD

This story is my diary of the compassions, emotions, and heart wrenching turmoil affecting American families during World War II. Little did I know at the time, I would play a role during the war that would bring some of the families, who didn't know the fate of their relatives missing in action, a sense of hope and faith that they may see their loved ones again.

At age 100, my memories of the war years are as vivid as they were seventy eight years ago, when our country went to war with the Axis powers. I have many specific recollections of those years, especially watching my husband leave for military service in Europe, and how I received information after he was wounded on the battlefield at the Battle of the Bulge. There are other experiences that brought tears to my eyes during the war when the mailman came to my door. I received Letters of Hope from prisoner of war family members, acknowledging the communications I sent them regarding the status of their husbands, sons, fathers, and brothers. Those personal memories have been kept in a box since the war ended in 1945. They are memories of American Airman that became prisoners of war when their airplanes were shot down over Nazi occupied countries.

This is the story of the contents of those postcards and letters and what I did to bring comfort to the families of loved ones, who fought and sacrificed their lives in distant lands for our country.

It is my hope you will share my emotions reading the words expressed by their family members, who lived every day of the war wondering if their loved ones were alive, while being grateful to receive word, any word, about the fate of their men.

Agnes Joan Negra

November 13, 2019

"AS LONG AS THERE ARE AMERICANS
LIKE YOU WHO ARE DOING SUCH WONDERFUL
WORK AND GIVING SUCH WONDERFUL SERVICE TO OUR FELLOW
AMERICANS, I'M SURE VICTORY WILL BE OURS, AND YOU CAN BE
SURE YOU AND OTHERS LIKE YOU HAVE PLAYED A VITAL PART"

MOTHER OF PRISONER OF WAR
TO AGNES JOAN NEGRA, JUNE 21, 1943

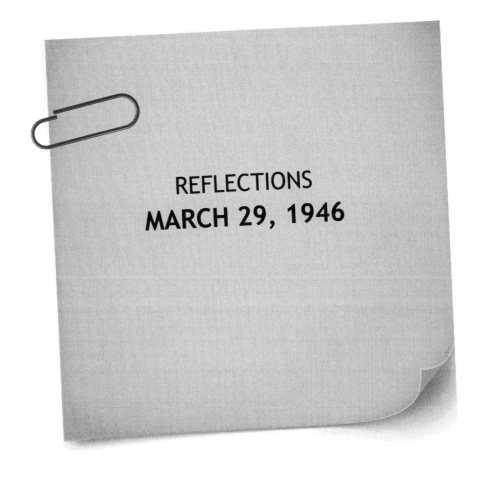

REFLECTIONS
MARCH 29, 1946

REFLECTIONS: MARCH 29, 1946
PENN STATION
NEWARK, NEW JERSEY

Yesterday, March, 29, 1946, my husband Gus, was honorably discharged from the Army at Fort George G. Meade, Maryland. When I received the phone call from him last night telling me he would be arriving home by train at Penn Station, Newark, I was so overjoyed by the news! However, emotional thoughts soon started racing through my mind. Would wounds show from his war injuries? Would our four year old daughter Pattie recognize him or even go to his outreached arms? How would he and I relate to each other? Would there be emotional scars from his combat experiences? I thought about what he must be wondering. How would he support his family now? What would be his emotional state, after being wounded in action in the Rhineland Campaign, left for dead, rescued and hospitalized for forty four days in an American hospital in newly liberated northern France?

These concerns kept me up all night. The next day, I woke Pattie at 6:00 am to get her ready for our trip to the train station. Gus' train was due to arrive at 11:00 am. My father-in-law Joseph Negra offered to accompany us to meet him. He, too, was worrying about seeing his baby son returning home from the war, after being on an emotional roller coaster, having two other sons Anthony and John in combat in the European and African theaters. The latter, and third oldest son John, parachuted from 14,000 feet, jumping from his B17 bomber after being shot down over Yugoslavia on November 7, 1944. Three months passed without any word from John, before my in-laws received a telegram advising he was missing in action. We didn't know John was taken as a Nazi prisoner before escaping German soldiers, with the help of the partisan Yugoslavian underground.

We arrived at Penn Station at 9:00 am. The weather was a typical dreary New Jersey March day with strong winds keeping the temperature in the low 30's. It started to snow, but there was sunshine in my eyes. I would soon be reunited with my husband. Penn Station was exciting as I glanced at the interior of the 1930's art deco building that I had only seen one time before, when we left for Atlantic City, on our honeymoon in September, 1941. Today, it was a bustling environment full of people from all backgrounds with one mission, greeting war weary American soldiers back home and to their families. I was amazed at the enormous number of men and women in uniform returning from war and traveling to points unknown. I got my daughter sitting comfortably on a bench, gave her a coloring book and crayons and was engrossed in listening to train arrivals being announced, while watching families cry and embrace their beloved soldiers as they emerged from the platforms, some of them were without limbs looking emotionally drained, but with tears of happiness on their faces.

Then it hit me like a bolt of lightening! Every person in uniform and their families had a story-a life altering experience since December 7, 1941. I realized, even though not intended, I may have played a role in the lives of some of these service people. Had I touched any of these lives? Were any of these American Army Airmen prisoners of war? I had a story also-not only of my husband and how our lives changed the day he entered the Army, but of the prisoner of war families I met after receiving over two hundred postcards and letters from them.

Then the Announcement came..."Attention those waiting for the arrival of the Fort Meade, Washington DC train, arriving at Gate 3." My husband was finally home!

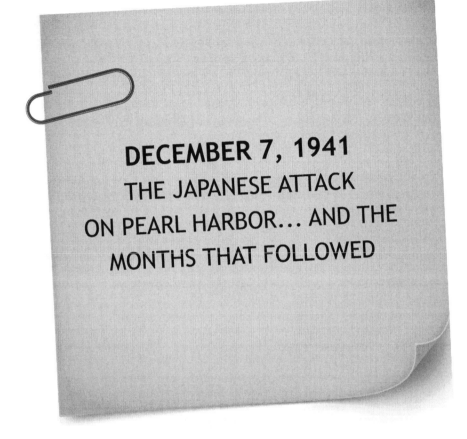

DECEMBER 7, 1941
THE JAPANESE ATTACK
ON PEARL HARBOR... AND THE
MONTHS THAT FOLLOWED

DECEMBER 7, 1941
THE JAPANESE ATTACK AT PEARL HARBOR
AND THE MONTHS THAT FOLLOWED...

"A date that will live in infamy" is a day all families alive on December 7, 1941 will never forget. That day instantly changed many lives. I remember where I was and exactly what I was doing when we heard the news bulletin on the radio that Sunday around 2:30 in the afternoon. Earlier that day, my husband and I attended the 11:00 am mass at Holy Family Catholic Church in our home town of Nutley, New Jersey; and, as was our custom at the conclusion of the service, we drove in our 1936 gray Ford a short distance to my in-laws home to join the Negra family for Sunday dinner. The temperature that day was clear but wind made the air feel colder and set the tone for the dismal news we were about to hear.

My husband, August, or "Gus" as his friends called him, was the youngest of four brothers and enjoyed sharing Sunday afternoon dinner with the entire family. This Sunday was a special day. He and I were married in September of 1941 and, my doctor, Anthony Caputo, had just confirmed in late November that I was pregnant. I too, had a news bulletin. Our plan was to announce the exciting news to the family after dinner. The oldest Negra son, Joe, had recently announced his wife was pregnant, as well. There was much to celebrate. My father-in-law's real estate and insurance business was enjoying success, all family members were healthy and were not negatively impacted by the depression, my in-laws would soon become grandparents, and the future was bright.

We were enjoying dessert after a delicious Italian meal. The brothers were sitting in front of the Philco radio set glued to station WOR, listening to the New York Giants versus Brooklyn Dodgers football game.

Yes, Brooklyn had a football team then sharing the spotlight with the famous Dodger baseball team. There was a short radio bulletin announcing the Japanese had bombed Pearl Harbor. We were stunned by the news, but surprisingly, the play by play of the game continued.

A neighbor knocked on the door and in an anxious voice told us to listen to CBS or NBC. CBS was broadcasting a concert from Carnegie Hall, but broke away announcing the large Naval base in Hawaii had been bombed with many casualties. Additional news bulletins were coming every few minutes with confusing announcements including Manila being bombed and the capture of a Navy gunboat off China by the Japanese Navy. Then came the worst news possible. The large U.S. Navy base in Hawaii was bombed by Japan. Every bulletin screamed despair and destruction after an unprovoked attack by Japan on our ships, air bases, and military. There was speculation about the number of American casualties on ships docked at Pearl Harbor and at airplanes stationed at Hawaii's small airfields. One news reporter reported fears of our west coast being invaded. We had no idea of the magnitude of the Japanese attack or that Hitler would immediately declare war on America. Our immediate thoughts turned to our young neighbors and friends, who were serving in the Navy. Were any of them in the Pacific fleet and on the ships at Pearl Harbor?

Everyone in the house was angry! My husband's brother, John, showed the most emotion. He had enlisted in the Army Air Corp on August 12, 1941 and was at home on a short leave that day. He knew his flight training would speed up his entrance into combat and was anxious to hit back at Japan; however, he soon discovered the Army Air Corp would quickly have targets in Nazi occupied territories in Europe and England and was desperate for American flyers. Brother Anthony declared he would immediately enlist in the Army. My husband, the youngest of the four brothers, spoke of joining the Navy after hearing of the large number of casualties inflicted on ships and seamen. He felt sailors would be needed immediately. I begged him, as did his parents, not to act on emotions and to remember I was only in the beginning stage of my pregnancy and not due to deliver our first baby until late August or September. The unknown soon became the most pressing thing on our minds. The President's wife Eleanor Roosevelt was the first government person to give a statement. After having our country divided for the past two years about supporting England or entering the war in Europe, she had the clearest radio message saying, "There is no more uncertainty." We needed, as a country, to unite and to rise above the crisis. Many Americans did not want to get tangled in another foreign war. Japan and Hitler soon changed their minds.

I was able to keep my husband from rushing on Monday to the Nutley Town Hall to "sign up." At least he waited for some time before he headed to the Navy recruitment station. In that period of time, several of his childhood and high school friends had enlisted and were waiting basic training orders. His best friend from childhood Walter Stecewicz was one of the first to enlist. We later received word that Walter was killed in action in Europe. My husband was devastated about Walter's death and carried a picture of him in his wallet throughout the war.
Our weekly town newspaper, The Nutley Sun, carried the names each week of Nutley boys missing or killed in action. Emotions ran high especially since our family knew most of them.

My husband was working in a manufacturing company that soon turned its equipment and technology into a defense plant. There was much confusion about the next steps for those men that were registered for the draft. Gus was registered. Would his job working in a defense plant delay his entry into the war? Would the government decide not to draft expectant fathers? Those questions were paramount on my mind.
My husband waited for the birth of our daughter Pattie who was born August 26, 1942, and then headed for the closest Navy recruitment office.

After a lengthy application process and testing period, he was rejected for service by the Navy. For the first time, he discovered color blindness was a vision deficiency in his life. He also had malaria as a teenager being infected during a visit to a popular picnic spot called Garret Mountain.

The Navy wanted no part of him, with the advice to go back to his family and await the notification from another service.
The Navy recruiter truly believed no other military arm would accept him because of his vision and malaria issues and questioned why his classification was 1A. I have to admit I was no patriot pleading with him to wait before enlisting. His fear was receiving a draft notice which would restrict his opportunities for selecting what he wanted to do in the military. My fear was being a widow. As required by a law passed in 1940, all men between 18 and 37 had to sign up for the draft. My husband was registered and classified 1A, physically fit for military service. Rumors and unanswered questions were part of our daily thoughts. Would men with

children be drafted? There was no immediate answer. The Navy rejection of him bought me some time and allowed emotions to ease.

The early news from the Europe and the Pacific theaters of war was not good. Whenever possible, my husband would stand in front of the Town Hall to hug his friends and wish them well as they departed for war. On a September day in 1942, his second oldest brother Anthony would be in that farewell group headed for the Army. He soon joined General George Patton's 7th Army in Africa in a tank division.

Gus was content to wait until the birth of his child, but wanted to get involved someway to help the war effort. He had a restless empty feeling knowing that so many of his friends were serving in the military. An elderly World War I veteran knew of his anxiety about watching his friends go off to war. One night, the veteran knocked on our apartment door and offered us a shortwave radio. He explained that he heard the German Army was cooperating with the Red Cross giving them the names and home towns of American Airmen prisoners of war. The Red Cross had arranged to announce the names on the radio every night at 6 pm. I thought, why not write down the names heard on the radio broadcasts and contact the prisoner's families to offer them comfort during their time of grief and sorrow? What resulted from our letters to the families was a totally gratifying experience for us and them.

As the war progressed throughout 1942, bad news occurred almost every week. My husband's family had deep roots in our home town of Nutley, NJ settling there in 1907. They were highly active in the town through civic activities, participating in town organizations that aided those residents in need, and in Holy Family Catholic Church.
My father in-law Joseph was on the Board of Directors of the Nutley Savings and Loan Bank, grantor of many of the home mortgages in the community.

The town was a small and close knit community with friendly people. As the saying goes, "everyone knew everyone." With four boys going through the local school system, being active in sports, and their father having a real estate and insurance business, the Negra family was well known and respected. News from the battlefront, usually negative, affected the family in a very personal way. In 1941, the Negra home had the distinction of having the only telephone on the street; therefore, news and communication was active since most of the sons, and then husbands on the street and in the neighborhood, were overseas serving in the military.

The Negra family home eventually had three stars displayed on a ribbon in the front window signifying the three boys serving in the armed forces. The second oldest Negra son Sergeant Anthony served in Patton's 7th Army in a tank command in the invasion of Africa and Italy. He then saw combat in the 3rd Army in northern France. Son, Staff Sergeant John, was a tail gunner in a B17 in the Army Air Corp flying and completing thirty-nine missions before his airplane was shot down during a bombing assignment over Maribor, Yugoslavia, where Nazi aircraft engines were manufactured. The youngest son, my husband, PFC August, was in Patton's 3rd Army serving in France at the Battle of the Bulge and in the Rhineland Campaign. Their objective was to liberate France and invade Germany with Berlin as their goal. Sons, John and August were wounded in combat, but returned home after the war.

My husband entered the Army in 1944. The time had come! I agreed he needed to do what was on his mind from the day Japan bombed Pearl Harbor. Working in a defense plant with other fathers and mothers was noble and needed for the war, but his commitment was to play a greater role. In a few months, his wish would come true as he was in combat in the Rhineland Campaign liberating France and fighting to defeat Germany.

My family, the Verdi's, originally from Boston, moved to Nutley in 1938 and operated a fish market at 187 Franklin Avenue, in the town's business center and on the main thoroughfare. Our family market was well known in town and the only place to purchase fresh fish and seafood. The store tagline was: "If it swims, we have it." I can still remember the long lines of customers on Friday afternoons extending out the door and down the street waiting to enter and ask my mother and father for their favorite fish. My family, also, had numerous relationships with people in town. My parents were on an emotional roller coaster having a son John serving in the Navy as a Petty Officer and a son seventeen year old Joseph in the Merchant Marine. We were constantly praying for their survival and safe return home.

Chief Petty Officer John was in an Navy espionage unit living in caves in the mountains on the coast of China. His mission was to report Japanese Ship movements to Navy Intelligence. His life was constantly in danger as Japanese Army units would locate his position forcing him and his Chinese guide to evacuate to a different cave. As the war progressed, he was rescued by an American Naval vessel that was eventually sunk by a Japanese kamikaze plane. Fortunately, John was rescued in the sea by another ship and survived. Marine Joseph crossed the Atlantic several times in the dangerous Merchant Marine service delivering arms and ammunitions to England and France. Due to their service responsibilities, we had very little communication from them. Frankly, we had no idea of the dangerous missions they were undertaking. I later read the Merchant Marine Service had the greater number of casualties on the sea. I wrote to my two brothers often not knowing if they received my letters.

As the calendar ended the first year of war, the public was ever conscious of bad news from Europe and the Pacific. We learned of island names never in our vocabulary and of places in Europe thought of as peaceful countries, but ravaged by war. Reports of casualties and prisoners of war occupied the headlines of newspapers. Families of the prisoners and those missing in action remained hopeful of good news; however, the predominant emotion was not knowing the fate of their loved ones.

The war touched every life. The unknown and fear for those we loved occupied our daily thoughts.

Information on the status of those men and women serving was scarce, and at times, nonexistent. Telegrams from the War Department containing sad news were delivered, in my town, by bicycle via a telegram employee. Neighbors would see that bicycle come down the street and panic praying it would not stop at their house. If the bicycle rolled up to another house, emotions would explode as everyone hastily ran to console their neighbor anticipating the arrival of bad news.

The world was consumed by aggression. England and the Allies were getting hammered by the Nazi war machine all over Europe with threats of the invasion of the United Kingdom mainland while Japan was marching and occupying one Pacific island after another with the strategy of building a line of defensive bases to protect the invasion of their country.

THE SHORTWAVE
RADIO

THE SHORTWAVE RADIO

As the pressures of war escalated on the families hoping to get information on the status of their family member not heard from in weeks or months, or those that were reported as missing in action, or listed as prisoners of war, the shortwave radio emerged as a potential link to provide some answers to those questions. Families were starving for news... any news of their loved ones.

I had heard of people in America having shortwave experiences listening to radio stations in Germany, Italy, Japan, Singapore, and Manchuria, but I had no knowledge of using the equipment. Americans were anxious to hear any news of the war even though our government always warned about Axis propaganda and false information. It was time for me to act.

In early 1943, a friend told me Radio Berlin was cooperating with the Red Cross and producing the names of American prisoners of war that could be accessed on a shortwave radio. Five names were released every night at 6 pm. The American prisoners spoke into a microphone giving their name, rank, date of capture, and the home addresses of their families. I immediately wondered, do the American people know of these broadcasts? Would the War Department or Red Cross notify the prisoner's families of this information? My answer was "of course," but I wasn't sure and soon discovered many prisoner of war families never received confirmation of the status of their family members from the War Department.

I became determined, and mastered the Shortwave equipment! I became a listener to studio announcers at stations in Germany. Frankly I was shocked, but surprised at the messages over the radio from American prisoners of war. Were they real? I listened at 6 pm to every broadcast and cared about only one thing...the names and addresses given of the prisoners. Should I take the risk of notifying the families their loved ones were alive with the chance the Nazi government was using the radio broadcasts to further punish American families and convince them to no longer support American involvement in the war?

We lived in an environment of warnings. "Be careful, don't believe what you hear."
Trust was under scrutiny every day of our lives.

At every opportunity, I listened to foreign broadcasts and jotted the names and addresses of every prisoner on the airwaves. Could I bring hope to a family that their son, husband, father or brother was alive?

With pen in hand, I wrote down names and addresses of prisoners held by the Germans. I penned individual letters to families all over the United States telling them the prisoner status of their loved ones.
My mission was set and in motion. I was proud to contribute a positive note to the war effort even though I had no idea if this effort would bring peace, faith, or hope to the families.

I knew my mission was a serious one and wanted the recipients of my letters to feel assured, though not fully knowing if the information I was relating was falsified by the Nazis. I was determined to be a reliable source of information. I decided to sign my letters with my husband's name feeling it would give them more credibility coming from a man.
Silly as that may sound in the current world we live in, women living in that time would clearly understand my well intentioned motive.

When I began my letter writing campaign and communicated to hundreds of families, I never expected to hear a response. I was mistaken. The emotional responses to my letters were many including postcard replies from all over the country. The penny postcard was the preferred way to communicate. More formal responses arrived in letters on company stationary from lawyers, businesspeople, and doctors. It didn't matter; everyone responding to my messages was desperately trying to find information of their loved ones who, in many cases, had not communicated with their families for several months. I became dedicated to documenting the names of American prisoners of war and communicating to their loved ones that their relatives were alive. The news from the battlefront was usually dismal, especially during the first full year of the war. American families, whose soldier's lives were uncertain, needed positive news. The American spirit in families was to think positive, but uncertainty ruled the day.

My letters all began the same way...."To the family of (name of family member), it is with my sincere hope I am giving you good news about the status of (name of family member). Through my shortwave radio, I learned from the Red Cross (name of family member) is alive and being held in a German prisoner of war camp. I pray for him and for your family that all of you will be reunited soon." I wrote over two hundred letters hoping that my words would bring some comfort to the families.

On November 7, 1944, my husband's parents received a telegram from the War Department, advising that their son John's airplane was shot down during a combat mission over Yugoslavia. It formally listed John as "missing in action." The Nazi's invasion and occupation of that small European country was known, so the fear of John's survival was very real. My thoughts immediately went to my Shortwave Radio. Was John alive?

Did he parachute safely? Was he a prisoner of war? Did the Red Cross have any of these answers? With a new, fiercer determination, I anxiously listened to broadcasts from Germany and other Axis countries on the shortwave, with the hope that John was a prisoner of war, and I would hear his name assuring our family he was alive. I never heard his name announced and thankfully he was rescued and survived the war.

POSTCARDS
AND LETTERS
OF HOPE AND
THANKS

POSTCARDS AND LETTERS OF HOPE AND THANKS

Three years ago while my son was asking questions about my husband's war records, I dug deep in a storage closet and discovered a box of letters and postcards that I received from prisoner's families. Not since 1945, had I investigated the contents or read the many postcards, letters, and family notes... There they all were. The cards written to me in 1943 and 1944 from the families of prisoners of war. The families I wrote to during the war advising them their loved ones were alive and being held in a prison camp. Their jubilant responses telling me the news from my letters was comforting to them. Some of my letters confirmed the brief information that had been communicated by the War Department, but others were elated that my notification was the first news they had received after not hearing from their soldier for weeks or months. They were ecstatic to hear their loved ones were alive. Their emotions expressed were a mix of anxiety, relief, fear, excitement, comfort, and hope.

As I read through the letters, I immediately had one regret-that I had not communicated with any of the families since my first contact. Did their loved ones survive? What became of their lives? I will never know.

I decided to publish some of the postcards and letters I received from the prisoner of war families during the war years. They clearly describe the emotions and turmoil World War II had on the soldiers, as well on their families. In Tom Brokow's book, they are called "The Greatest Generation." How true.

To my amazement, many of the families I contacted responded with their grateful appreciation, with postcards, letters, and in some cases, pictures of their prisoners of war.

As I read those remarks after receiving them over seventy five years ago, they brought tears to my eyes. Those same emotions are with me today even though the responses represent a place and time long ago.

The very first postcard I picked up and read that day with my son, convinced me that these messages from prisoner of war families needed to be shared.

On June 21, 1943, Mrs. W H Smith of Elizabethtown, Pennsylvania, a prisoner of war mother whose son was in a prison camp and received my letter, expressed her feelings the best:

"As long as there are Americans like you who are doing such wonderful work and giving such wonderful service to our fellow Americans, I'm sure victory will be ours, and you can be sure you and others like you have played a vital part."

June 21, 1943

Dear Sir,

I want to thank you for writing me that you heard through short-wave from Germany my Son Staff.Sgt. C. Smith was a Prisoner of War. Thirty some persons heard this Broadcast & wrote me either letters or cards A few days later the U.S. Government verified this announcement and my son is a Prisoner of War.

As long as there are Americans like you who are doing such wonderful work and giving such wonderful service to our fellow Americans, I'm sure Victory will be ours, and you can be sure you and others like you have played a vital part.

I want to thank you for both myself and my son.

Gratefully Yours,

Mrs W. H. Smith

THIS SIDE OF CARD IS FOR ADDRESS

Mr. A. Negra
67 Harrison Street
Nutley, New Jersey

I am delighted to share, in the following pages, the actual heartfelt post-cards and letters I received from Mothers, Fathers, Daughters, Sisters, and Family members as they shared their anxious emotions upon hearing or confirming their loved ones were prisoners of war. Many are relieved to know their soldiers are alive as they struggle to live the next months or years with the unknown. I wish every response could be included, but there are far too many.

Rarely, a week went by when my mailbox didn't contain a postcard or let-ter from a mother or father of a prisoner of war. I read their comments with great emotion hearing them speak of the role their son had as an Army Airman Pilot, Navigator, Gunner, or Crew Member. They were sor-rowful, but full of pride.

Note: I tried to translate the words expressed by the respondents as they were written; however, due to penmanship, there are examples of names that may not be correctly spelled or words that are unclear.
I apologize for any errors.

On May 7, 1943 Albert Mac C. Barnes of New York wrote:

"Please pardon the delaying answering your communication about my son, First Lieutenant William S. Barnes.
The news of his safety was like a happening of a miracle after five weeks of extreme anxiety.
Mrs. Barnes and I wish you to know how fine and generous hearted you were to put yourself out for one you did not know. We take pride in the belief that your unselfish act typifies the spirit of good Americans toward one another.
It may interest you to know that today I have received confirmation of your information from the United States War Department.
Very truly yours, Albert Mac. C. Barnes"

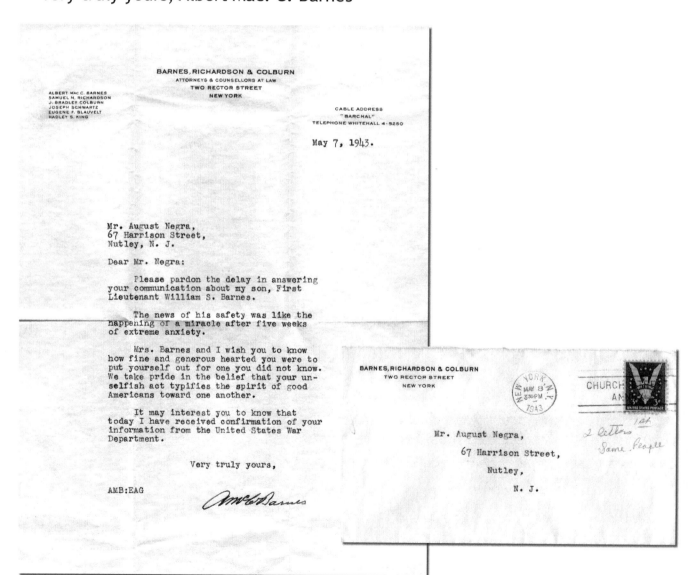

On April 21, 1943 Mrs. Frank Wiench of Dickinson North Dakota wrote:

"Thank you much for the information about our son, Lt. Alfred Wiench now a prisoner of the Germans. It was very kind of you to write us. We are very happy to know that he is alive. To show our appreciation for your charitable act I am enclosing a nuns apostle prayer.
Sincerely, Mrs. Frank Wiench"

On April 30, 1943, Mr. Arthur Weldon from Lowell, Massachusetts wrote:

"I wish to thank you most sincerely for your kindness in relaying the information you received over radio concerning my son Lt. Arthur J. Weldon, Pilot, who was reported missing in action in Africa March 26th. It is a great relief to know he is alive. Gratefully Yours, Arthur P. Weldon"

Mrs. S.T. Johnson of Los Angeles wrote on May 4th, 1943:

"I wish to thank you for your kindness in writing me the news that 1st Lt. Franklin T. Johnson 0659715, my son, is a prisoner in Germany. We received word March 30-43 that he was missing in action, and had no other news. He flew a P40-Pursuit Plane. The news he was alive was surely wonderful to receive. May the Lord bless you in your acts of kindness to people who have loved ones missing. Prayer does wonderful things. Yours truly, Mrs. S.T. Johnson"

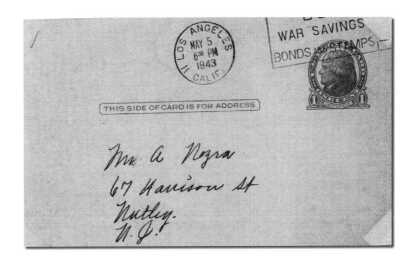

On July 23, 1943, Mrs. Willis Campbell of East Liverpool wrote:

"I don't know how to thank you. My son has been missing since June 13. He was a pilot on a Fortress so I can never repay you for your card telling me he was still alive. So I just hope and pray for God to bless you and thanks again. Mrs. Willis Campbell"

On May 15, 1943, Mrs. D.A. Sipe of Pittsburgh, Pennsylvania wrote:

"Lt. Harry D. Sipe is my son and a navigator on a Fortress. He has been missing since April 17 over Bremen. Your message has made us so very happy. Just to know he is alive is such a relief. We certainly appreciate your kindness in notifying us. Gratefully, Mrs. D.A. Sipe"

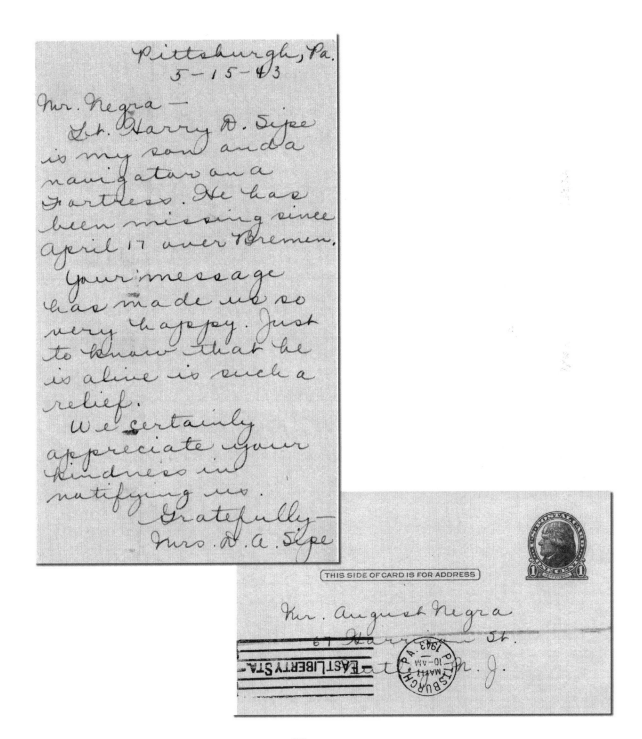

On June 13, 1943, Thomas Daly of Stoughton, Massachusetts wrote:

"Thank you for your kindness in forwarding information concerning short wave from Germany in which you heard Francis M. Daly's name as a prisoner of war. We were very glad to know of his whereabouts as he had been missing in action. Yours very truly, Thomas Daly and Family"

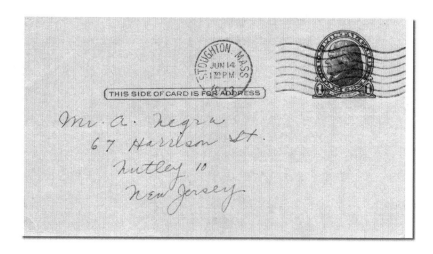

On June 1, 1943, M Stafford of Ballston Spa New York, wrote:

"Thank you so much for your kind message. I did not hear the broadcast and had had no good news of my husband for some time. Consequently, you may realize what great relief your card brought and how much I appreciate it. Sincerely, M. Stafford"

On May 15, 1943, Mrs. Jack O. West of Ottumwa, Iowa wrote:

"I would like to thank you for sending along the information you received via short wave concerning my husband, Capt Jack O. West.
Since receiving your card, we have been officially notified that he is a Prisoner of War. Your kindness is greatly appreciated. Sincerely, Mrs. Jack O. West"

On June 13, 1943, Mrs. John W. Lawrence of Salisbury, Maryland wrote:

"Thank you for your kindness in writing me about the news of my brother Staff Sargent Ralph C. Farr being a prisoner. It is correct. It makes me happy to know he is alive and hope he returns soon. Respectfully yours, Mrs. John W. Lawrence"

On June 12, 1943, Mrs. Russell of Gary, Indiana wrote:

"I want to thank you for notifying me that my brother Sgt Peter Brasic was a prisoner of war at Germany. Yours was one of eight letters I had received saying they have heard he's a prisoner. As yet, I have not received a official notification to this effect. So you must know how much the letters have meant to me. Thank you"

On June 17, 1943, Mrs. Forrest Hughes of Sacramento, California wrote:

I am indeed grateful for the news of my husband, T/Sgt Forrest S. Hughes. This card of thanks can hardly show the extent of my appreciation for your effort in getting this message to me. It was difficult to bear this feeling of loss upon receipt of the previous report that my husband was missing in action - one often imagines the worst. Your card brought a relief for me hard to express in words. We have received confirmation of your report. Many, many thanks. Sincerely, Mrs. Forrest Hughes"

On May 22, 1943, Mr. and Mrs. Edwin C. Shurig of Richmond Heights, Missouri wrote:

"Thank you so m much for letting us know our son Lt. Robert C. Shurig a pilot on a B-17 Flying Fortress out of No. Africa is alive although a prisoner of war in Germany. Sincerely yours, Mr. and Mrs. Edwin C. Shurig"

On May 29, 1943, Mrs. L.P. Williamson of Wilmington, North Carolina wrote:

"Many thanks for the information about my son. Any other news will be appreciated concerning him,
we didn't hear the broadcast. Sincerely, L.P. Williamson".

On July 12, 1943, Mrs. Gus Martin of Patterson, California wrote:

"It is with deep appreciation that we have received your card. Many others have been kind, as you have been. We have thought our son to be probably killed by now, and you can imagine what a God-send the broadcast was. It seems almost too good to be true. I would give so much if every mother could receive this news instead of the other. The Provost Marshall General has not verified the statement yet, but it gives us new hope. Thank you for your kindness. Sincerely, Mr. and Mrs. Martin"

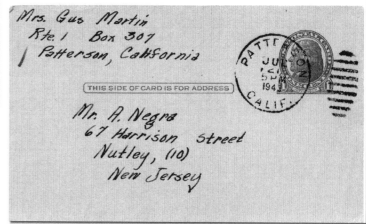

On May, 22, Mrs. William Archer of Milwaukee, Wisconsin wrote:

"I hasten to thank you for the good news you relayed to us in regard to Staff Sgt Gordon M. Archer #20645968. We had feared the worst since learning from Washington that he was missing in action in the No. African area. You should be happy to be the bearer of such good news to anxious relatives. Let me thank you again. Mrs. William Archer"

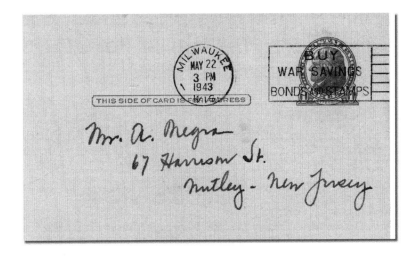

On May 1, 1943, Mrs. C. Kindle of New York City wrote:

"I want to thank you for the information concerning my son, S/Sgt Charles F. Kindle who was reported missing April 4. It was a great comfort to hear this news; that he is still alive. Thanks Again. Sincerely, Mrs. C. Kindle"

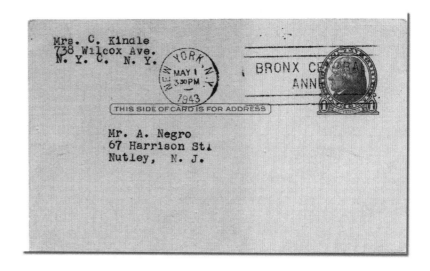

On May, 8, 1943, Ivan A. Boyce of Olean, New York wrote:

"First Lt. Newton Boyce was shot down in Africa Jan, 24. On Feb 7 came the Gov. telegram reporting him missing in action. On Feb 28 a gentleman in Canada wrote he heard the German radio report him a prisoner of war which was indeed good news which he sent Feb 9. The 2nd German broadcast of him on April 22 was good news and recent. I have read 38 reports of it so far. You are doing a very fine work and I sincerely thank you from the bottom of my heart. I shall be glad to write you at greater length if you are interested. Yours very truly, Ivan A. Boyce"

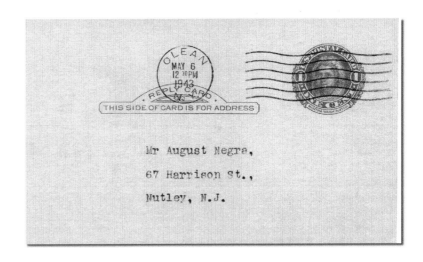

On June, 24, 1943 Mrs. J. F. Croush, Sr of Columbia, S.C. wrote:

"I appreciate your writing me that my son is a German prisoner.
Thank you for your kindness and thoughtfulness. Mrs. J. F. Croush, Sr"

On June, 7, 1943 Mrs. Hazel Benson of Hartford, Connecticut wrote:

"Thank you very kindly for being so thoughtful as to send me that very helpful and thoughtful information concerning my son Earl. The news greatly relieved my anxiety. I have since heard from Washington receiving his full address. I haven't heard from Earl yet, but I pray each day I shall. If you hear anything further, please let me know. In deep appreciation, Sincerely, Mrs. Hazel Benson"

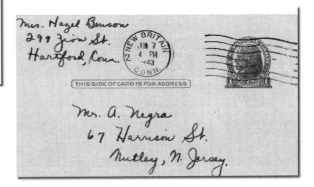

On July 6, 1943 Mr. and Mrs. Fred Stelzer of Celina, Texas wrote:

"Many thanks for writing to our daughter in law at Dallas and letting us know about the short wave message that my son, Sgt James B. Stelzer was trying to get through from Germany. We had a letter from him saying that he was all right. We have four sons in the service: James B. a German prisoner, Sgt William Stelzer in New Guinea. Ralph Stelzer a.o.m. second class U.S.N. and S/Sgt Harold F. Stelzer with the Sig. Rad.Int. If at any time you pick up a message from any of them would be so glad if you could let us know. Sincerely again many many thanks. Mr. and Mrs. Fred D. Stelzer"

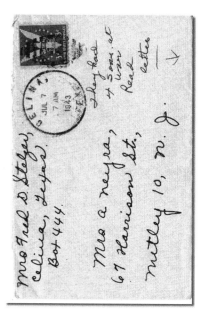

On June, 9, 1943 Mrs. Clyde Covert of Michigan wrote:

"Your card was one of about 50 that came telling of hearing Howard's name as a prisoner of war. Maybe you would be interested in knowing he was a radio man in the Bomber Ferry Command. About the time he was reported missing, another son was killed in action in Africa. You can imagine how low both Mr. and Mrs. Covert were feeling and sure needed something to give them a lift in spirits. Well all those letters from strangers did what friends and family had failed to do. Mr. and Mrs. Covert both are in war work and just don't have the time to answer so many letters in a reasonable time, so I'm helping, I am a sister of Mrs. Clyde Covert"

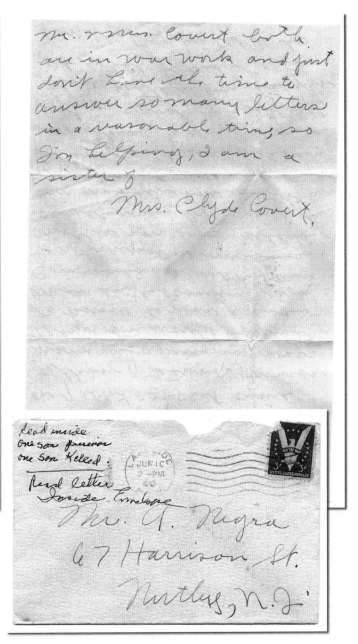

On June 28, 1943 Mrs. E. Dobsa of New York City wrote:

"I wish to acknowledge and thank you for your card informing me of my son, 2nd Lt. Albert Dobsa, prisoner of war in Germany. I received a letter from him the other day saying he had recovered from the slight injuries received and is now at a camp. He said the food is good and they are well taken care of. I also have 3 other sons serving in the armed forces. Thank you again, Mrs. E. Dobsa"

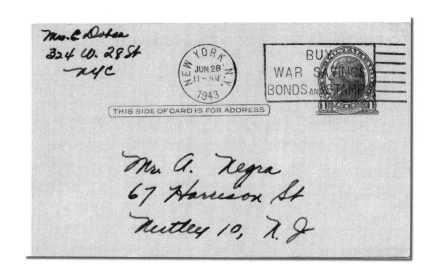

On May 19, 1943 Mrs. Alfred J. Lippincott of Trenton, NJ wrote:

"Thank you so much for notifying me of the german short wave broadcast concerning my son P. of W. It is indeed a splendid service you are rendering to anxious parents. Thank you again. Mrs. A. Lippincott"

On May 19, 1943 Mrs. Margaret Campbell of Fulton R.D.4, NY wrote:

"Many thanks for your card reporting about my son S/Sgt Theodore W. Campbell. It makes me very happy to know he is alive and can now be looking forward to seeing him again and I hope it won't be long. Thanking you again. I am wishing for Victory. Mrs. Margaret Campbell"

On May 29, 1943 Mrs. E. S. Gulick of Washington D. C. wrote:

"I want to thank you ever so much for the time and trouble you took to send me information about my husband. Mrs. E.S. Gulick"

On May 11, 1943 Mr. and Mrs. M. Schmidt of Vineland, NJ wrote:

"We received your card and was glad to hear the news. Although our Son is a prisoner we at least know that he is alive and well. We want to thank you very much for your kindness in informing us about our Son. We also heard it in the radio last night. Alfred has also received the Air Medal and Single Oak Cluster for his part in the invasion of Africa. Sincerely, Mr. and Mrs. M. Schmidt"

On June 28, 1943 Mrs. Aug Wandtke (unknown location) wrote:

"Please excuse my tardiness in answering your thoughtful message concerning the whereabouts of my son T/Sgt Gilbert Wandtke. I hope that this short note of thanks will spur you to continue your practice and bring relief to other fear stricken mothers. Yours truly, Mrs. Aug Wandtke"

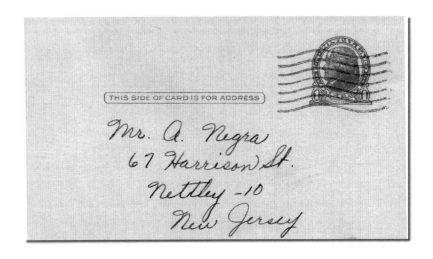

On May 23, 1943 Mrs. Frances Romme of Philadelphia, PA wrote:

"Thanks for the kind thought in informing us that our Son Lt. Harold Romme is a prisoner of war. There are kind and good people on this earth who try to inform heart sick parents of their Son's whereabouts. May God bless you and keep you well so you may continue to inform other worried parents. Gratefully, Mrs. Frances Romme"

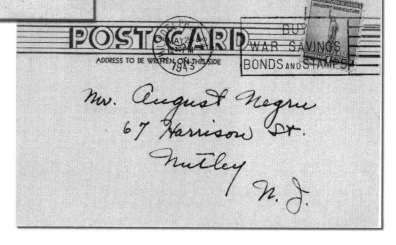

On May 22, 1943 D. Hill and Family of St Augustine, FL wrote:

My family and I greatly appreciate your card and the other notices we received from various states concerning our son 2nd Lt. Raymond D. Hill, Jr 0-731068 who had been missing since April 4th in the North Africa area. Although we had our official notice from the government stating he is a prisoner in Germany, it makes us very happy to know so many are interested in relieving our anxiety. Sincerely, D. Hill and Family"

On June 20, 1943 Mrs. Mary Ruth Winchell of Southport Indiana wrote:

"Thank you for telling me you heard the name of Lt. John Winchell on the short wave broadcast from Berlin. The War Department notified me June 11 that my husband is being held prisoner in Germany, but I did not hear the broadcast. I appreciate your kindness in sending me this information. Very truly yours, Mrs. Mary Ruth Winchell"

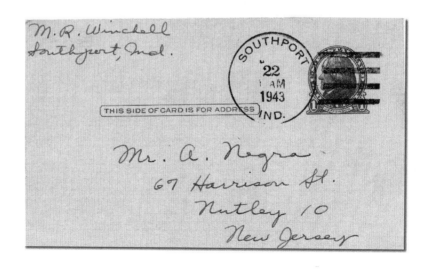

On May 29, 1943 Mrs. O.H. Klaas of Seattle, Washington wrote:

"Thanks for your card letting us know abut the broadcast on which our son's name was mentioned. We were notified by the War Dept last Monday that Lieut Klaas was a prisoner of Germany and was wounded when captured. He was shot out of the skies over Tunisia on April 6th and we hope someone with a short wave will be able to catch a message direct from him. He had previously been reported captured by the Italians. We appreciate your letting us know. Sincerely, Mrs. O.H. Klaas"

On May 26, 1943 Mr. Messeun of Newark, New Jersey, wrote:

"Your postal received and thanks for the same. You and many more have written me and it sure was appreciated. All of these cards and letters, I am keeping for my son when he comes home with the help of God. He is only a kid and is in the service 26 months. To be exact he is only 20. He is a tail gunner. Well thanks again. I remain, Mr. Messeun".

On October 30, 1943, Mr. and Mrs. J.C. Emrich of Louisville Kentucky, wrote:

"Thanks very much for your kindness in notifying us that on Saturday, April 24, the Berlin radio announced that our son, Vincent, was a prisoner of the German government. We were previously notified of his capture by the Adjutant General at Washington. We deeply appreciate your kindness in writing us and will welcome any additional message you hear concerning him. God willing we anxiously await his return. Sincerely, Mr. and Mrs. J.C. Emrich"

Louisville, Ky.,
April 30, 1943.

Thanks very much for your kindness in notifying us that on Saturday, April 24th, the Berlin radio announced that our son Vincent was a prisoner of the German Government. We were previously notified of his capture by the Adjutant General at Washington. We deeply appreciate your kindness in writing us and will welcome any additional message you hear concerning him.

God willing, we anxiously await his return.

Sincerely,

Mr. and Mrs. J.C. Emrich

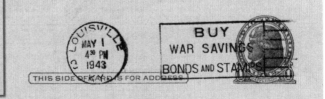

On July 20, 1943, Mrs. Ruth M. Wolte, of Hagerstown, Maryland, wrote:

"Just a few words letting you know I appreciate this message very highly and also I have received a letter from my boy on the sixth of July, too. It surely makes a person feel good to hear such good news. My son was commissioned a second Lt. Navigator in the Air Force. I thought you would like to know what rating he stood. I thank you both. Yours Truly, R.M.W.

On June 27, 1943, Emma Cranford of Emmett, Idaho, wrote:

"It was very grand of you to take that much of your time to let me know about hearing of S/Sgt. Roland Magee being a P.O.W. and many thanks to you. Roland was reported lost 5th of April and just the day I had received a letter from him in Stalog Germany and was I glad and then your card. I got 31 cards telling me it is grand to know there are so many kind and thoughtful people left in the old world. Roland is an orphan and I am his nearest of kin. I am his Aunt, my only boy so you know how I feel to you and all. May God Bless you for your kindness..
Very Truly, Emma Cranford R.D. #1"

On June 1, 1943, Wesley Wood of Bartlesville, Oklahoma wrote:

"We wish to thank you for your kindness in sending us the information about my brother Lt. Harold Wood of Lexington, Oklahoma. He had been missing in North Africa since April 5th and has been officially declared a prisoner of war. As we seem to be unable to contact this shortwave station, any further information which you may hear will be greatly appreciated. Wesley Wood"

On August, 30, 1943, Mrs. M.J. Cody of Reno, Nevada, wrote:

"My daughter in law sent me the card you wrote her when you picked up the shortwave broadcast telling of the capture of Capt. W.E. Cody. That was very kind of you to write and we appreciate your kindness very much. We have received both letters and cards for Capt. Cody. He says he is well and that they are well treated. Also says the Red Cross do a great deal for them. Again thanking you. Very Sincerely, Mrs. M.J. Cody".

On April 22, 1943, Dr. and Mrs. C.M. Barnwell of Atlanta, Georgia, wrote:

"We wish to express to you our sincere appreciation for writing us about the broadcast of our son, Lt. Charles M. Barnwell. It was most helpful and encouraging, though we had been notified by the War Department that he was a Prisoner in Germany. Sincerely, Dr. and Mrs. C.M. Barnwell".

On May 31, 1943, S.W. Rhodes of Redley, California, wrote:

"I want to thank you for notifying me of the broadcast about my son being a prisoner in Germany. The War Department has confirmed this. I appreciate your interest, again I thank you. Sincerely, S.W. Rhodes".

On May 19, 1943, L.D. Highsmith of Gesup, Georgia, wrote:

"Your card received in regards to the German Broadcast stating my son William Troy Highsmith Staff Sargent was prisoner of war in Germany I think very kind of you to write me about this. Thank you so much L.D. Highsmith".

On June 12, 1943, Mrs. Ed Smith, of Avondale, North Carolina, wrote:

"I received your card of May 29 and "thank you very much for it". I heard my son, Clyde from Berlin back in April. Sincerely yours, Mrs. Ed Smith".

On July 22, 1943 Edw. Dostie of Newmarket, New Hampshire, wrote:

"Many thanks for the information which you have sent me concerning my son T/Sgt. Edward J. Dostie we appreciated receiving your card as some-one else wrote and told us they heard the Broadcast and with two telling us about it we are doubly sure that he's there. Many Thanks. Yours truly, Eds. Dostie".

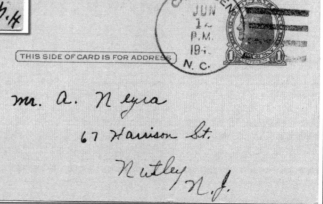

On July 14, 1943, Mrs. Lee of San Antonio, Texas, wrote:

"Dear friend. Many thanks for your card informing me of safety of my son Robert in Germany. Had a card from him dated May 24. Have his address so I hope to hear from him soon. He is so loved. Has one year service was Radioman Gunner of B24. His two brothers and father in service. Sincerely yours, Mrs. Lee".

On May 14, 1943, John Mc Donnell of Brooklyn, N.Y. wrote:

" Yours was among the many letters received telling us the good news of our son, and brother. You certainly have taken a great load off our minds and hearts. As we had only known that he was "Missing in Action". If it had not been for the kindness of so many strangers we would not yet know his fate. We all wish to extend our heartfelt gratitude and thanks. We also feel that we will always be deeply indebted to you".

101 Berkeley Place
Brooklyn, N. Y.
May 14, 1943

Dear Friend,

Yours was among the many letters received telling us the good news of our son, and brother.

You certainly have taken a great load off our minds and hearts, as we had only known that he was "Missing In Action". If it had not been for the kindness of so many strangers we would not yet know his fate.

We all wish to extend our heartfelt gratitude and thanks. We also feel that we will always be deeply indebted to you.

Sincerely,

John Mc Donnell

On April 30, 1943, Mrs. S. Jerome Allen of Edmonton, Alberta, Canada wrote:

"Thank you very much for your card letting us know of this report you picked up about my brother, Harry F. Swanson, Staff Sgt. We have known since February that Harry is a German prisoner but it is a comfort to receive these cards telling about these messages as we have only received one letter from him since his internment. If you receive any more reports in regard to Harry we would be so happy if you will let us know. Harry was a gunner on a B17 Fortress. Thank you again for your interest in sending us this report. I am, sincerely yours, Mrs. S. Jerome Allen".

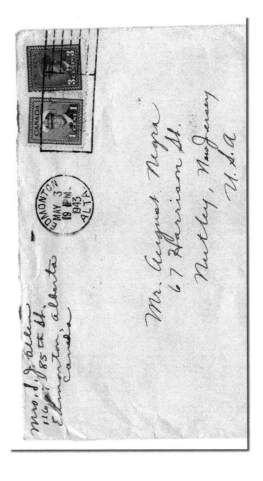

On May 4, 1943, Mr. and Mrs. Robert Abercrombie of Fay, Oklahoma wrote:

"Want to thank you for your card of April 29, 43 telling about Arley Abercrombie being a prisoner in Germany. Arley had to bail out in Italy but had been transferred to Germany. He was a member of a B17 crew. Have never heard from him but have heard of him through the War Department. Thanking you again, we are respectfully yours, Mr. and Mrs. Robert Abercrombie".

On April 28, 1943, Frances C. Bowman, of San Diego, California, wrote:

"Thank you so much for letting us know about hearing the German broadcast of our son, Horace D. Bowman, a prisoner of war- we had been notified by the War Department and last week we received a letter from Horace himself from Germany where he is interred. Apparently the Germans are treating their flyer prisoners pretty well, and while it is not a happy situation we feel very grateful to have him alive. Sincerely, Frances C. Bowman".

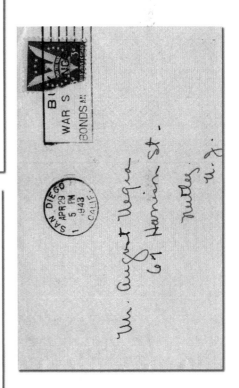

On June 17, 1943, Mrs. R.S. Callaghan, of Bloomfield, New Jersey, wrote:

"Thank you so much for relaying the news of my husband, Lt. Richard S. Callaghan. I have received over forty letters from all over the country and truly appreciate everyones thoughtfulness. No one can understand the horrible feeling of anxiety unless they lived through it themselves. The telegram stating my husband had been missing since May 15th arrived on the 24th of May. This was followed by an official notification that he is a prisoner, June 11th. My sincerest thanks for your kindness. Sincerely, Betty H. Callaghan".

On June 17, 1943, Walter Lally, of St. Paul, Minnesota, wrote:

"I want to thank you for the card concerning the shortwave broadcast of the prisoners of war. We were officially notified that our son was a prisoner several days previous to this broadcast. He had been missing since April 17th and we were greatly relieved with that information. Thank you again for your thoughtfulness. I remain yours truly, Walter Lally".

On May 13, 1943, Hazel M. Ewing of North Baltimore, Ohio, wrote:

"Your kind message was received telling of the whereabouts of my son, Warren James Ewing, and I wish to thank you sincerely for your thoughtfulness in sending this message to me. I have not yet heard directly from the government that Warren James is a German prisoner, but have received over 70 letters and cards from various people telling me that the also heard the broadcast. In closing, let me again express my thanks to you. Sincerely yours, Hazel M. Ewing".

May 13, 1943

Mr. A. Negra
67 Harrison Street
Nutley, New Jersey

Dear Mr. Negra:

Your kind message was received telling of
the whereabouts of my son, Warren James
Ewing, and I wish to thank you sincerely
for your thoughtfulness in sending this
message to me.

I have not yet heard directly from the
Government that Warren James is a German
prisoner, but have received over 70 letters
and cards from various people telling me
that they also heard the broadcast.

In closing, let me again express my thanks
to you.

Sincerely yours,

Hazel M. Ewing

Hazel M. Ewing

Mr. A. Negra
67 Harrison .

Nutley, New Jer.

On June 6, 1943, Mrs. Hugh A. Boyd, of Wheeling, West Virginia wrote:

"Just a line to let you know we appreciate your kindness in writing us about Hugh A. Boyd. Your may be interested to know we received 21 cards from folks who heard the broadcast. His mother and I thank you again. Sincerely, Mrs. Hugh A. Boyd".

On July 3, 1943, Floella Duzan of Terre Haute, Indiana wrote:

"Please forgive the delay in answering your card, believe me I do appreciate it. I have heard from my son and am calming down to the social obligations to the 30 nice, lovely friends who sent word of my son, 1st Lt. Haldon R. Haywood. I thank you in behalf of both of us. Floella Duzan".

On July 23, 1943, Mr. and Mrs. B.W. Webster, of Crawfordsville, Indiana wrote:

" We wish to thank you for the card telling us you heard our boy's name S. Lt. Robert Webster on broadcast. We have not yet received his address Sincerely Mr. and Mrs. B.W. Webster".

On May 27, 1943, Charles Randall, of Wheatland, Wyoming wrote:

"My dear friend, I cannot find words enough to express my appreciation of the information concerning my son S/Sgt. Charles Eldon Randall. I received the message April 23 that he was missing April 17. I received 58 letters and cards of his whereabouts. Thanking you again for this valuable information. Sincerely, Charles Randall".

On May 1, 1943, Mr. R.H. Wilson, of Youngstown, Ohio wrote:

"I have received your very interesting card and wish to thank you for it. I got a telegram February 13 telling me that he was a Prisoner of War. We have also heard from him since and he said he was well and safe. I'll close now thank you Respectfully, Mr. R. H. Wilson".

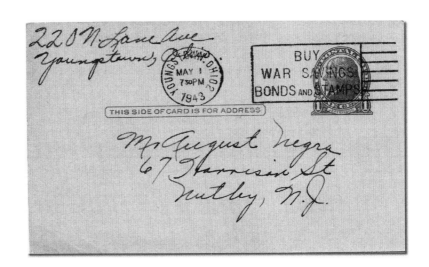

On June 15, 1943, Mr. and Mrs. C.B. Caruso, of Clairton, Pennsylvania wrote:

"Thank you very kindly for the message of our son. He has been a prisoner since July 13, 1942. It was broadcast in August also. Sincerely, Mr. and Mrs. C.B. Caruso".

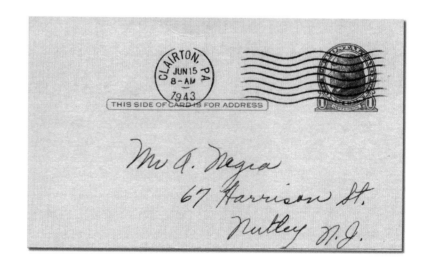

On June 28, 1943, Mrs. B.J. Lovin Sr. of Allen, Oklahoma wrote:

"I received your card last week. Thank you so much. I heard from my son Saturday he is well and okay. Would appreciate it very much if you would write me if you hear any news in the future. May God Bless you. Mrs. B.J. Loving Sr".

On May 25, 1943, H.F. Hayes of Mirror Lake, New Hampshire wrote:

"I would like to thank you for the card sent concerning Francis D. Bowles. I am very grateful and know that all of the other families that you have rendered this service to must feel the same. Sincerely, H.F. Hayes"

On August 12, 1943 Mr. and Mrs. M. M. Huschle of Eden Valley, Minnesota wrote:

Your card date July 20 telling of your listening in on short wave Berlin broadcast and informing us that they announced Staff Sergeant Lawrence J. Huschle prisoner of war of the German government. Words fail in saying how much this news meant to us. To know our son Lawrence was alive. He was reported missing June 13th. We also had a card from another short wave listener a few days ahead of your card. This last week we received the official from the War Department. Again words fail us in expressing our grateful thanks for sending us the information.
Enclosed find $1.00. A small sum to help towards the expense of keeping up your good work. Sincerely, Mr. and Mrs. M. M. Huschle"

Some of the begining of their letter was fading; so I wrote the rest of it out in this paper.

Starting with the line. To know our son Laurance was alive. He was reported missing June 13th. We also had a card from another Short Wave listiner a few days ahead of your card. This last week we received the offical from the War Dept.

Again words fail us in expressing our gratefull thanks for sending us the information.

Inclosed find $1.00 small sum to help towards the expence of keeping up your good work.

Sincerly
Mr + Mrs M.M. Huschle
Eden Valley,
Minnesota

M.M. Huschle
Eden Valley Minn

EDEN VALLEY
AUG 13
2 PM
1943
MINN

Mr A. Negra
67 Harrison St.
Nutley 10. Newark
New Jersey

On June 19, 1943 Mr. and Mrs. Fred Lambert of Marinette, Wisconsin wrote:

"Thank you for your kindness in informing us of the whereabouts of our son who is a German prisoner. The number of cards received giving this information surely shows the sympathy people feel for the parents of our boys in service in their anxiety. Seventy-five people notified us since Ji-une 16th. We are sending a snapshot of our son. It was taken while he was at home on a furlough last March. Gratefully yours, Mr. and Mrs. Fred Lambert"

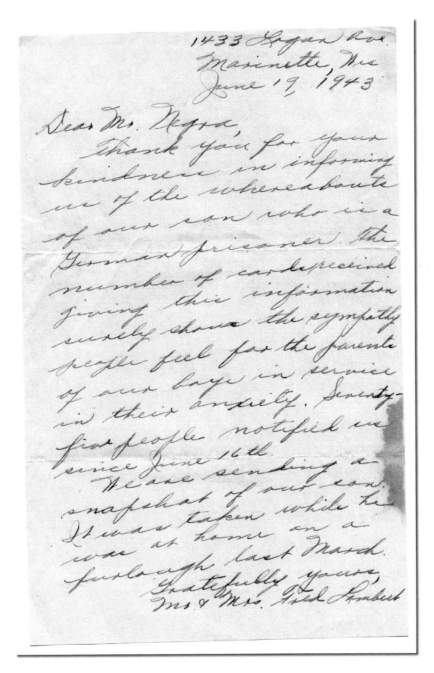

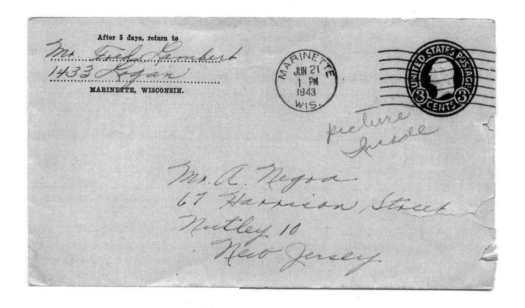

After 5 days, return to

Mr. Fred Lambert
1433 Logan

MARINETTE, WISCONSIN.

MARINETTE
JUN 21
1 PM
1943
WIS.

UNITED STATES POSTAGE
3 CENTS

picture
inside

Mr. A. Negra
67 Harrison Street
Nutley 10
New Jersey

S/Sgt. Aloysius N Lambert
1433 Logan ave
Marinette, Wis

3 4

On May 12, 1943 Edwin Consolmagno of Boston, Massachusetts wrote:

"I wish to thank you for writing to me giving me the news of my son 1st Lieut. Joseph E. Consolmagno. I had been notified over a month ago that he was missing so you can understand how relieved we feel now.
Assuring you that my wife and I appreciate your kindness, I am, Yours very sincerely, Edwin Consolmagno".

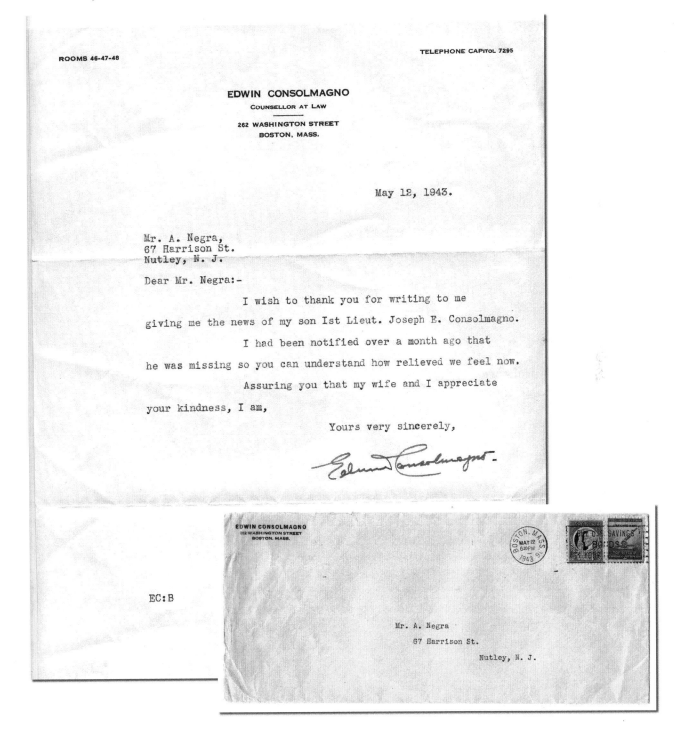

On May 14, 1943 Mrs. Drake of New York, NY wrote:

"I want to thank you for your kindness in letting me know of the where-abouts of my husband, 1st Lieutenant Nicholas R. Drake, who is now a captive in a prison camp in Germany.
I had received word that he was missing in action in North Africa and I as-sure you that your message was very welcome. Now my mind is at ease in regard to his welfare. Sincerely, Mrs. Drake"

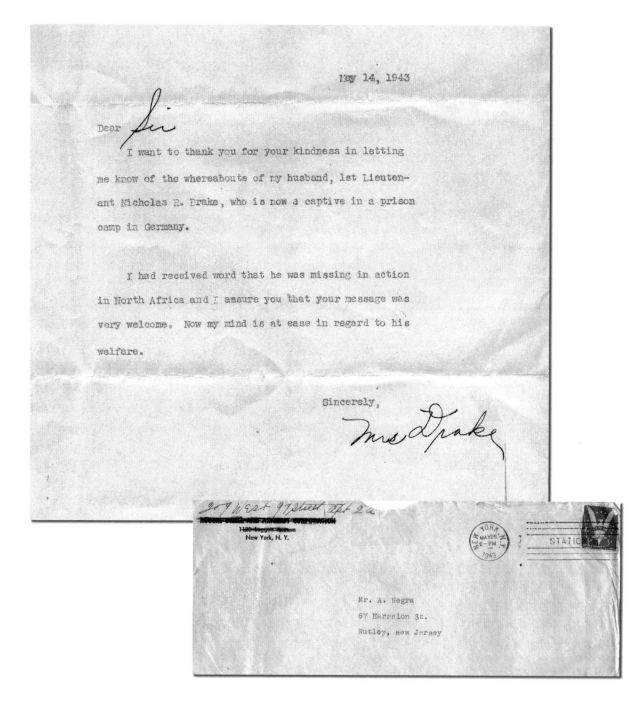

On May 14, 1943 J. C. Wilson of Milwaukee Wisconsin wrote:

"You were good enough to write to us and tell us of a short wave broadcast you picked up on the evening of May 6th from Berlin announcing that
our son Tom is a prisoner of war of the German government.
Tom was probably co-pilot on a medium bomber in the North African ter-
ritory. He was reported missing as of April 5th. You can realize that we
were very much relieved to know that he is still alive.
If you happen to pick up any further messages from him or references to
him in these broadcasts, we would very greatly appreciate a letter or col-
lect telegram from you. Tom's complete name, number and next of kin
are as follows: 2nd Lt. Thomas B. Wilson.
You will know that we very deeply appreciate your message and we know
that other families to whom you send similar messages will very much appreciate them. Very sincerely yours, J.C. Wilson"

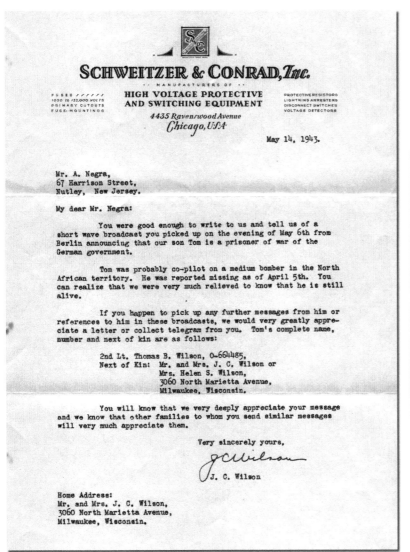

On June 7, 1943 Mrs. A. John Gallagher of Hollywood, California wrote:

"Received your most grateful notice informing me of Lieut. Earle J. Dumont's capture and well being.
Thank you very kindly for your sincere consideration, Mrs. A. John Gallagher"

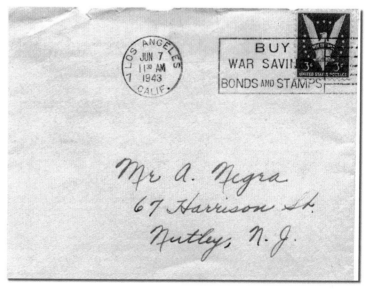

On June 13, 1943 Mrs. Anna Ostheimer of Lafayette, Indiana wrote:

"I am more than grateful for the card you sent telling me of hearing about my son being a prisoner of Germany. I have already received close to fifty such messages and I am thankful for each and everyone of them. If at anytime you hear more as to his whereabouts or condition I wish you would drop me a line. The War Department has not been able to verify this message as yet.

No one knows the anxiety that we are living in from day to day. At times these things seem unbearable, but we will surely be blessed with victory and a just peace.
Thank you again for the interest that you have shown, I remain, Sincerely yours, Mrs. Anna Ostheimer"

This is an example of a Prisoner of War Father reaching out for a friend whose son is missing in action with no notification as to his whereabouts or if he is alive:

On October 19, 1943 Albert Mac C. Barnes of New York, NY wrote:

"You very kindly notified me in April, 1943 of the receipt of a short wave radio message from Berlin advising of the taking of my son, William S. Barnes, as prisoner. It may interest you to know he is in a German person camp and we have heard from him a number of times.

Mr. friend, Alfred T. Brady of 300 Lydecker Street, Englewood, N.J., has been informed that his son, Joseph C. Brady, has been missing in action since sometime in September. Perhaps you are still listening to the short wave broadcasts, and if so, will you be good enough to advise Mr. Brady if you hear anything concerning his son. I have sent a copy of this letter to Mr. Brady. Sincerely yours, Albert Mac C. Barnes"

On May 3, 1943 Mrs. W. B. Ligett of Middletown, Ohio wrote:

"We have received several hundred letters from people all over the country who have heard over short wave that our son 1st Lt. Robert Eugene Ligett #0659730 is a prisoner in Germany.
He has been in combat as a fighter pilot in Africa for over 5 months. He has been missing in action since March 26th.
On April 24th we received an unofficial report from the War Department saying he was a prisoner of the Italian Government. So far this has not been verified.
It is such a relief to know he is still alive.
Thanking you for your kind interest in our son. Sincerely, Mr. W. B. Ligett"

On May 17, 1943 Mr. and Mrs. Wigham of New York, NY wrote:

"We thank you sincerely for your kind and welcome message that our son, Reginald, is a prisoner in Germany.
We are very happy to learn that he is alive.
Many other kind people have sent us a similar message.
Sincerely, Mr. and Mrs. Wigham"

We thank you sincerely for your kind

and welcome message that our son, Reginald,

is a prisoner in Germany.

We are very happy to learn that he

is alive.

Many other kind people have sent

us a similar messgage.

Sincerely,

Mr. and Mrs. Wigham

May 17th, 1943.

Mr. August Negra,
67 Harrison Street,
Nutley,
New Jersey.

On June 6, 1943 Ruth Johnson of Frederick Town, Ohio wrote:

"My family joins me in expressing our gratitude to you and many others for the cards and letters sent us in regard to my brother, 2nd Lt. Richard S. Johnson. We think it very kind of you to take the time to write these messages.
We had received a telegram from the war department that he was a German prisoner of war but had no information as to where he was being held.
Richard was a B-25 Mitchell bomber pilot in the North African area but we have never received any details as to what might have happened. Thanking you again, Very Sincerely yours, Ruth Johnson"

On June 24, 1943 Roy N Berg of Loxahatchee, FL wrote:

"Thank you for informing me that August Ullrich is alive and uninjured.
Gus, as we call him, came to work for us three years ago. His parents are dead and he was raised in an orphans' home in New York.
He left here to enter the service thirteen months ago and was trained as a waist gunner on a Flying Fortress. He is a conscientious and determined boy and made an excellent soldier. We accounted for at least three or four German Planes and received three decorations.
It is unfortunate for us that he is out of the picture for the duration.
Yours very truly, Roy N. Berg"
Palm Beach-Loxahatchee Co.
Owners and Developers of Citrus Grove Lands

On April 21, 1943 James A. Brown of Spokane, Washington wrote:

"I am writing in receipt of your letter of April 16th concerning German broadcast on prisoners.
We received a letter from our son a week ago Saturday stating that he was a prisoner in Germany, but it is certainly nice of you to write us in this manner and I want to tell you that we appreciate it. Thanking you, I am, Yours very truly, James A. Brown"

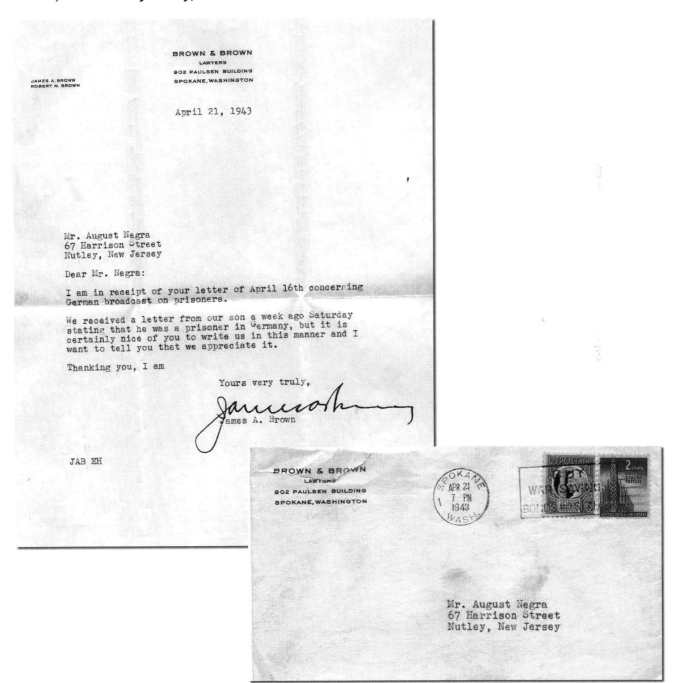

On July 18, 1943 Mrs.. Hartley Westbrook of Coon Rapids, Iowa wrote:

"May I take this means of thanking you for your card regarding the short wave broadcast in which you heard that my husband was a prisoner of war in Germany.
I have been a long time in acknowledging your message due to the fact that many others heard the broadcast and wrote me also. I am grateful for each of them. I have received four letters from him and he seems to be getting along fine. I am so thankful.
May I again extend my sincere thanks to you. Mrs. Hartley Westbrook"

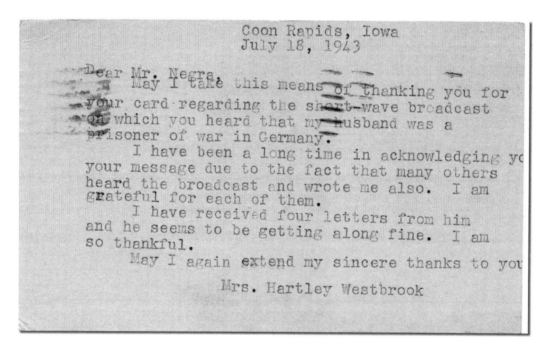

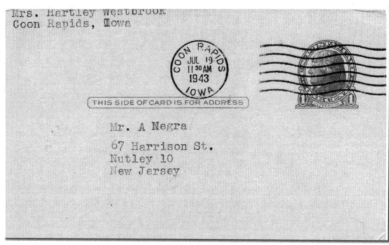

On June 7, 1943 Lorraine K. Ross of Dayton, Kentucky wrote:

"I received your card about the German broadcast you heard in which my husband, 1st Lt. Kelly G. Ross, was reported a prisoner. I received such word from the War Dept. on May 17.
To date, I have received 29 cards and letters like yours.
I greatly appreciate your thoughtfulness in writing me. Sincerely, Lorraine K. Ross"

207 - 6th Ave.
Dayton, Kentucky

Dear Mr. Negra:

I received your card about the German broadcast you heard in which my husband, 1st Lt. Kelly G. Ross, was reported a prisoner. I received such word from the War Dept. on May 17.
To date, I have received 29 cards and letters like yours.
I greatly appreciate your thoughtfulness in writing me.

Sincerely,

Lorraine K. Ross

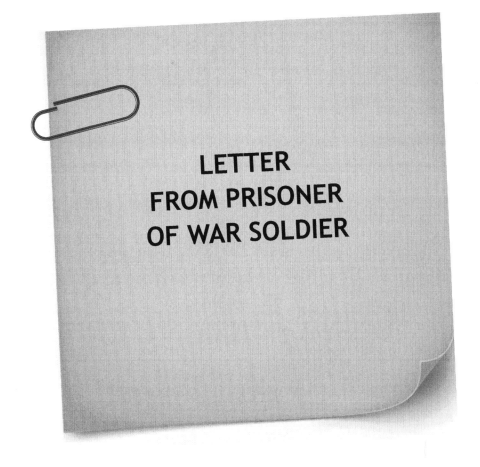

**LETTER
FROM PRISONER
OF WAR SOLDIER**

LETTER FROM PRISONER OF WAR AIRMAN
SERGEANT LAWRENCE HIRSCHLE, EDEN VALLEY, MINNESOTA

Even though I cherish every postcard and letter of appreciation I received in response from my correspondence to the Prisoner of War Families, my most treasured letter was written to me from an American Prisoner Airman that survived, was liberated from a Nazi prisoner camp, and returned home prior to the end of the war, to his Mom and Dad in Eden Valley, Minnesota. I had never received a response or any other type of acknowledgement from a prisoner of war soldier. Only from their families.

When Sergeant Hirschle returned home, the soldier was shown the letter I wrote to his parents in 1943 when I heard of his capture and prisoner of war status.

On August 15, 1943, Army AirCorp Sergeant Lawrence Hirschle wrote:

"Dear Mrs. Negra,

I shall try to express my appreciation for the message you sent the folks at home in 1943 when I hit a bit of bad luck. But your message helped the folks a great deal.

I was liberated on May 2, 1945 and came back to the states on June 13, 1945 and got my leave to come home started the 15 of June until the 19th of August...and now I report to Miami Beach for medical care and reclassification and etc.

The folks are all very fine now and that the war is suppose to be over. Maybe all the boys will be coming home a little more often even though we will have to maintain a large army for our own good.

Once again, i shall thank you from the bottom of my heart for what you did for the folks."
Sincerely,
Lawrence

Aug. 15, 1945

Dear Mr. C. Negra,

I shall try to express my appreciation for the message you send the folks at home in 1943 when I hit a bit of hard luck. But your message helped the folks a great deal.

I was liberated on May 2, 1945 and come back to the states on June 13, 1945 and got my leave to come home started the 15 of June until the 19th of Aug. and now I report to Miami Beach for medical care and reclassification and etc.

The folks are all very fine now and that the war in suppose to be over maybe all the boys will be coming home a little more after. Even through we will have to maintain a large army for our own good.

Once again I shall thank you from the bottom of my heart for what you did for the folks.

Sincerely
Lawrence.

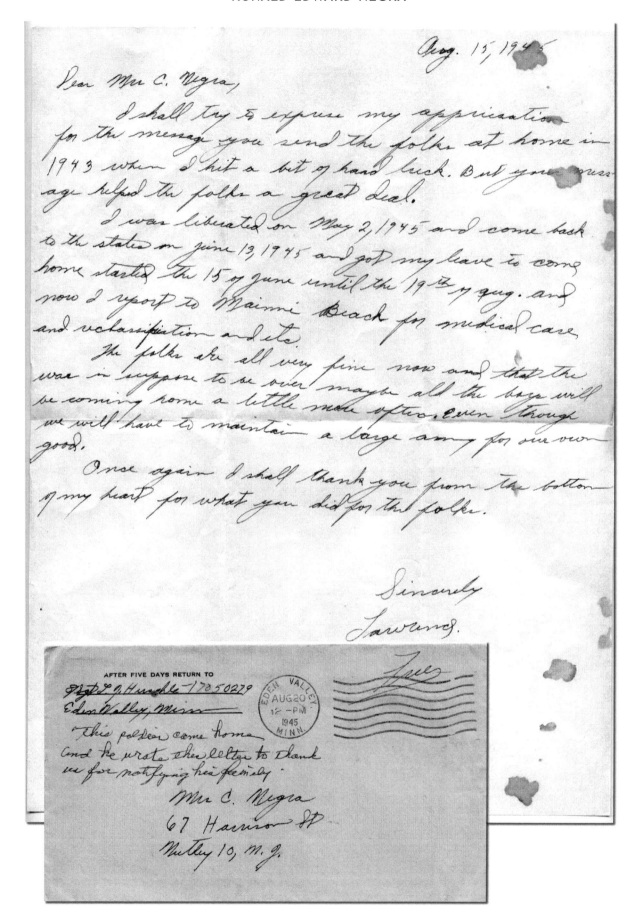

MY STORY

MY STORY

As I continued to listen to the prisoner of war broadcasts, I too, looked forward to letters from my husband. I didn't know Gus' actual location, but believed he was in combat somewhere in France. Our devoted mailman, Mr. McMann, was a kind, older gentleman emotionally charged when he saw a letter from a soldier to a family on his delivery route. He knew the Negra family and was welcomed into their home for a goodie every now and then. He loved my mother-in-law's chocolate chip cookies and had a wonderful relationship, often sharing her emotions having three boys serving in the military in Europe.

His excitement, with postal letter in hand, was a welcome sight. His trademark was the whistle he would blow to alert the family there was a letter from their soldier. Hearing that whistle, to me, meant my husband was alive.

Beginning in March, 1945, I didn't hear that whistle for over two months. I feared the worst; however, there was no word from the War Department. I rarely slept wondering if my husband was injured and alive. My days were consumed with emotions that ran from hope to emptiness, but I was a person of faith and knew Gus was a survivor and would return home to his wife and daughter. No letters arrived. My husband's parents tried to hide their emotions knowing their son John's life might have been lost somewhere in the farms of Yugoslavia, and now their baby son, Gus, was presumed to be missing in action.

I continued to listen to my shortwave radio and record the names and addresses of prisoners. I would reread the responses from mothers, fathers, wives, and sisters about their missing relatives continually reminding myself of their anxieties and sacrifices.

And then on a Tuesday afternoon in early May, there was Mr. McMann blowing his whistle. It was a letter from a nurse in the American 95th Hospital, located in Bar Le Duc, France. Mr. McMann and I were jumping up and down like we just inherited a million dollars. Then reality set in. The letter was written in French. I had no idea of its message. Then I remembered Gus had two years of the French language in high school and always praised his French teacher Helen Gerdnick. I needed a translator and Miss Gerdnick was that person. I raced to Nutley High School and discovered from Miss Gerdnick's translation that Gus was recovering from wounds received at the Battle of the Bulge. He had been hospitalized for forty four days at that hospital and asked the nurse to communicate to me in a letter dictated by him. Due to security and censorship, the letter was limited to letting me know he was alive and recovering from injuries. He was released from the hospital on May 4, 1945, but could not tell me if or when he would be coming home.

After receiving the letter from France, I stopped writing letters to the families of prisoner's of war. The broadcasts of names had ended.

It would be ten months later that Gus was discharged and returned home from Europe. I would then hear of the terrible ordeal of his combat wounds and experiences, of the Belgium underground partisans that saved him, and of the Belgium family that nursed his wounds before bringing him to a hospital in newly liberated northern France.

Of the five men from our families, the Negra brothers, Anthony, John, and Gus; and the Verdi brothers, John and Joseph, all returned home safely at the conclusion of the war. Our families were blessed to know all of these men served in combat on land and on the sea.

I do have one regret from the war years regarding the communications I received from the prisoner of war families. I often wondered if their soldiers survived the interment in the prison camps and if they lived through the remainder of the war. Did they see their families again?
I did think of contacting them, but was concerned about their privacy and desire not to discuss the war experiences they endured. I knew my husband never wanted to talk about the war, but participated for many years in veterans organizations assisting those men and women that were in need of mental health or financial assistance. Many veterans, like him, desired to move on with their lives looking at a positive future.

I may not know the answers to any of these questions, but I do know for sure that I was there, at a time when I was needed, using short wave radio and pen and paper, to deliver WAVES OF HOPE to these prisoner of war families.

Photo taken in France on May 4, 1945 of PFC August E. Negra after he was wounded in the Battle of the Bulge and released from the 95th American Hospital located in Bar Le Duc, France

GUS' STORY

GUS' STORY

These are my husband's words when he returned from the war:

"I was wounded in battle in March, 1945, while fighting to take control of Mannheim, Germany. My company was spread so thin in the Rhineland. It seemed at times we were lost, and frequently encountered splintered German soldier platoons that often resulted in hand to hand combat. Germans were firing 88 rounds at our position. As I took cover behind a building, an 88 round struck the building, throwing me about twenty feet in the air. My head and body ached something terrible and my nose, ear, and mouth were bleeding. Prior to losing consciousness, I remember seeing my entire platoon dead. I was told by two men that identified themselves as partisans, that as they were searching the bodies, they heard me moaning. They nursed shrapnel wounds to my back and arm. They feared the Germans would find me alive, so they took me to their home in Fontaine L'Eneque, Belgium, to a family named Lambillotte. Their address was Rue De Ahin-126 Ben-Ahin.

The family provided a hiding place for me while I regained consciousness and recuperated. I was told by a Belgian doctor that I suffered from a severe concussion, back injuries, and internal bleeding. Due to the damage to my back, I was unable to walk without assistance. I feared for the Lambilotte family's safety, and told the underground that I needed to get to American lines and medical help. They got me to the 95th General Hospital in Bar Le Duc, France, where I was hospitalized for 44 days and then released on May 4, 1945. After my release from the hospital, I was assigned to an ordinance battalion in France until the end of the war, when I returned home to my wife and family."

ACKNOWLEDGEMENTS

This book would not be possible without the many hours of interviews and discussions with my mother, Agnes Joan Negra.

To capture her memories of World War II and to appreciate how the war impacted the families of American Prisoners of War has forever been etched in my mind. All of these conversations with my mother were done with a goal of secrecy to be able to write this book without her knowledge. My objective was to complete it in time for her 100th Birthday Celebration on November 13, 2019.

I am forever grateful to my wife Valerie Negra for her counsel and advice in this writing, and for always being by my side throughout the challenges of keeping me focused while putting pen to paper.

Other family and friends were there to encourage me to write the book reminding me of the historical value it documents and to provide information confirming its content.

My grateful appreciation to Pattie Lerner, Adele Higgins, Ron Sterling, Judi Negra, Ed Negra, my late cousin Annette Verdi Zadotti, Jay Myer, and to Carol Comins for her creative expertise in the development of the cover of the book.

The author and his sister, Pattie, circa 1951, in front of the original shortwave radio used by Agnes Joan Negra.

ABOUT THE AUTHOR

Ronald Edward Negra, a Nutley, NJ native, was born on November 9, 1947. He enjoys writing about genealogy and wrote his first book in 2004 titled, "The History of the Verdi Family...Celebrating 100 Years in America." Ron also completed a book on the Negra Family History and on the life of his Father, August E. Negra.

Ron holds a Bachelor of Science Degree and a Masters degree in Business Management and Marketing. He retired as an Executive after working in the medical industry.

Ron was inspired to write "Waves of Hope" by his mother Agnes Joan Negra after learning of her extraordinary role in World War II communicating with the families of American soldiers as they were captured and became Prisoners of War. His mother always believed it was important for Americans to understand the sacrifices of these men and the emotions they and their families experienced of fear, anxiety, sadness, and hope.

Ron is married to his wife Valerie and lives in New Jersey.

Made in the USA
Middletown, DE
15 December 2020